HOW CAN I GRIEVE TO
GOD'S GLORY?

✖CULTIVATING BIBLICAL GODLINESS

Series Editors

Joel R. Beeke and Ryan M. McGraw

Dr. D. Martyn Lloyd-Jones once said that what the church needs to do most of all is "to begin herself to live the Christian life. If she did that, men and women would be crowding into our buildings. They would say, 'What is the secret of this?'" As Christians, one of our greatest needs is for the Spirit of God to cultivate biblical godliness in us in order to put the beauty of Christ on display through us, all to the glory of the triune God. With this goal in mind, this series of booklets treats matters vital to Christian experience at a basic level. Each booklet addresses a specific question in order to inform the mind, warm the affections, and transform the whole person by the Spirit's grace, so that the church may adorn the doctrine of God our Savior in all things.

HOW CAN I GRIEVE TO
GOD'S GLORY?

RYAN M. MCGRAW

REFORMATION HERITAGE BOOKS
GRAND RAPIDS, MICHIGAN

How Can I Grieve to God's Glory?
© 2019 by Ryan M. McGraw

Reformation Heritage Books
2965 Leonard St. NE
Grand Rapids, MI 49525
616-977-0889
orders@heritagebooks.org
www.heritagebooks.org

Printed in the United States of America
19 20 21 22 23 24/10 9 8 7 6 5 4 3 2 1

ISBN 978-1-60178-733-0
ISBN 978-1-60178-734-7 (e-pub)

For additional Reformed literature, request a free book list from Reformation Heritage Books at the above regular or e-mail address.

HOW CAN I GRIEVE TO
GOD'S GLORY?

Christians often struggle with how to grieve. Some believers feel guilty when they grieve because they know that they should rejoice in the Lord always (Phil. 4:4). Others use grief as an occasion to say, like Job, "God hath overthrown me" (Job 19:6). Yet there is a better and more biblical path to follow. Before I married my wife, Krista, I suggested that she and I memorize Lamentations 3:1–39. This passage furnished us with the necessary tools to grieve biblically by faith during later trials.

In the past ten years, we have experienced betrayal by friends, threats against our family, slander and gossip, and other forms of persecution. We lost our first child to miscarriage and our fifth child at the beginning of the last trimester (our little girl's face is still vivid in our memory). We experienced many of these things during a move that took us three thousand miles away from friends, family, and all that we knew. We lost property in the move. When several close family members died around the time of the move, we were prevented from attending most of their funerals. When we moved to our current home in 2015, we had personal health issues, one son in the hospital and another son requiring multiple surgeries, while hospitals refused repeatedly to work with our insurance company. In these trials and others, the words of Christ rang true: "In the world ye shall have tribulation: but be of good cheer; I have overcome the world" (John 16:33). As my family's experiences demonstrate, this life is often a vale of tears. Christ was a man of sorrows and acquainted with grief (Isa. 53:3), however, and the servants are not greater than their Master.

Lamentations 3:1–39 shows us how to grieve in a godly manner and how to exercise joyful faith in Christ simultaneously. In this passage, Jeremiah teaches us how to express sanctified grief (vv. 1–18), and he illustrates how to exercise faith in God under hardship (vv. 19–39). Because this is a lengthy passage, readers will be better helped as they read this booklet if they have Lamentations 3:1–39 in front of them. Part 1 of the booklet shows us how to grieve in a sanctified way, and part 2 demonstrates how to exercise faith under hardship.[1] The third part applies these and other scriptural principles to grieving over the loss of a loved one in Christ. We will see that it

---

1. These first two sections are adapted and edited from Ryan M. McGraw, "Walking Through Grief by Faith: Lessons from Lamentations 3:1–39," *Puritan Reformed Journal* 8, no. 2 (July 2016): 5–14.

is important to express rather than repress our grief, and we will learn how to do so by walking with Christ through our sorrows by faith.

FIVE BIBLICAL WAYS TO EXPRESS GRIEF

In Lamentations 3, Jeremiah outlines at least five ways God's people can express grief. He also gives them divinely inspired channels through which to express their grief before God.

God's Displeasure (v. 1)

The first thing to note is that Christians can express grief in a sanctified way. We are Christians and not Stoics. We trust in the Lord rather than resign ourselves to our fates. Lamentations 3, together with the Psalms, directs our grief through holy channels in prayer. Jeremiah experienced the terrors of Babylonian exile. The atrocities of the Babylonians were exceeded only by the depraved backsliding of the Israelites. Perhaps the evidence of this was that women ate their children in the famine that resulted from Babylon's desolation of Jerusalem (Lam. 2:20; 4:10, in light of Deut. 28:53). Lamentations 3 brings the themes of the entire book to their highest expression and resolution by teaching us how to express grief in a godly way.[2] The lament over the destruction

---

2. John L. Mackay, *Lamentations: Living in the Ruins* (Fearn, Ross-shire, Scotland: Mentor, 2008), 123.

of Jerusalem in chapter 1 now shifts to the prophet's personal lament.

The first verse of this chapter teaches us to acknowledge God's wrath. God is angry with the sins of His people, though they are not under His wrath as the wicked are (Ps. 6:1; 38:1). Christians must remember that such wrath is the displeasure of a Father who loves us and not of a judge who condemns us (Heb. 12:3–11). While like Jeremiah we may not always suffer for our personal sins, we must remember that all suffering is a result of Adam's fall into sin and that all suffering should lead to repentance from sin. Individuals often suffer for the church's sins and God's general judgments against it as well (Dan. 9:3–7, 6–15). Remember in your prayers that the Father may discipline us severely in love like an earthly father disciplines a child who is a repeat offender.

Hard Providences (vv. 2–7)

Believers experiencing trials are tempted to remove all restraints and complain against God. Job said,

> Though I were perfect, yet would I not know my soul: I would despise my life. This is one thing, therefore I said it, He destroyeth the perfect and the wicked. If the scourge slay suddenly, he will laugh at the trial of the innocent. The earth is given into the hand of the wicked: he covereth the faces of the judges thereof; if not, where, and who is he? (Job 9:21–24)

Job rightly acknowledged God's sovereignty even while he slandered God's character. Jeremiah gives us an alternative.

The expressions of sanctified grief in Lamentations 3 are diverse, and the writer's experiences are generalized in order to connect us to the text more effectively.[3] Do we feel as though we walk only in darkness (v. 2)? Are we troubled because we know it is God's hand behind our suffering (v. 3)? Do we feel our troubles in our bones (v. 4)? Is life bitter to us (v. 5)? Is our burden heavier because we see no way to escape (vv. 6–7)? Such expressions in Lamentations teach us how to pray and to sing the Psalms as well. We pray, sing, and meditate on this on God-given paths rather than wandering in the darkness on our own. We should learn to use laments and imprecations in Scripture to keep our sorrow within biblical bounds because biblical expression is better than free expression. We must voice complaints to God rather than against God. We must have brutal honesty in prayer coupled with a loving submission to our Father's hand.

Unanswered Prayer (vv. 8–13)

God commanded Jeremiah to stop praying for the people (Jer. 7:16; 11:14; 14:11). The problem was that he prayed for their prosperity regardless of whether they repented. This should make us ask how we pray

---

3. Mackay, *Lamentations: Living in the Ruins*, 125.

for our own countries. Do we pray for the stability and continuance of a land regardless of the character of its people? Sometimes we are frustrated because in spite of our prayers, it seems as though nothing goes right and nothing gets better. We feel as though God has torn us apart like a lion or a bear. While the Lord always gives abundantly more than we can ask or think (Eph. 3:20–21), the answers to our prayers often do not turn out as we expect. We must learn to sing by experience, "Teach me the patience of unanswered prayer."[4]

Persecution and Hardship (vv. 14–17)

All who desire to live godly in Christ Jesus will suffer persecution (2 Tim. 3:12), but persecution may take varied forms. We may be subjected to ridicule (Lam. 3:14). In these circumstances, we may be tempted to become full of bitterness (v. 15). We may be broken with grief and restless and forget prosperity (vv. 16–17). In verse 16, "He hath also broken my teeth with gravel stones," means looking in vain for food.[5] Sometimes we eat our bread with sorrow or forget our food entirely (Ps. 102:9). Like Jeremiah, we may find that our memories of past blessings may intensify our distress by exacerbating the bitterness

---

4. George Croly, "Spirit of God, Descend upon My Heart," in the public domain.

5. Mackay, *Lamentations: Living in the Ruins*, 133.

of the present.[6] Rather than stifling such thoughts immediately, we must release the pressure by venting them before God in a godly way.

Confessing Our Weakness (v. 18)

The prophet concludes this section of his lament by saying, "My strength and my hope is perished from the LORD" (Lam. 3:18). While this is never true for believers absolutely (Deut. 31:6; Josh. 1:5; Heb. 13:5), it is often true relatively, and even for a long time. We cannot give people the false assurance that the world gives by telling each other that everything will be alright. In Christ, we are more than conquerors through Him who loved us (Rom. 8:37). Yet cancer may take our lives. Persecution may increase. Our prayers for the spread of the gospel may come to fruition only after we pass from the scene, though these prayers will not fall to the ground. We must remember as Paul did and ultimately as Christ did that the Lord says, "My strength is made perfect in weakness" (2 Cor. 12:9).

How Should We Grieve?

The five occasions for grief find their highest expression in Christ's afflictions (e.g., Ps. 22:1–20; Isa. 53). We can exercise sanctified grief only when we exercise Spirit-wrought faith in Christ and experience fellowship with Him in His sufferings (Phil. 1:29;

---

6. Mackay, *Lamentations: Living in the Ruins,* 135.

3:10). Christ's cry, "My God, My God, why hast thou forsaken me?" was an act of faith and an expression of sorrow at the same time. In faith, He called God His God. In sorrow He cried, "Why hast thou forsaken me?" John Calvin wrote wisely,

> There is no one of the godly who does not daily experience in himself the same thing. According to the judgment of the flesh, he thinks he is cast off and forsaken by God, while yet he apprehends by faith the grace of God, which is hidden from the eye of sense and reason; and thus it comes to pass, that contrary affections are mingled and interwoven in the prayers of the faithful. Carnal sense and reason cannot but conceive of God as being either favorable or hostile, according to the present condition of things which is presented to their view.... When such a perplexing thought takes entire possession of the mind of man, it overwhelms him in profound unbelief, and he neither seeks, nor any longer expects to find a remedy. But if faith come to his aid against such a temptation, the same person who, judging from the outward appearance of things, regarded God as incensed against him, or as having abandoned him, beholds in the mirror of the promises the grace of God which is hidden and distant.[7]

---

7. John Calvin, *Calvin's Commentaries* (Grand Rapids: Baker Books, n.d.), 4:358.

This paints a realistic picture for grieving Christians. Christ was forsaken and bore God's wrath against sin so that we should no longer be children of wrath (Eph. 2:3). Christ trusted in the Father so that we might become the children of God (1 John 3:1–2). This means that Christ has sanctified our deepest trials and distresses to us so that they no longer express the wrath of a dreadful judge to us, but the loving hand of a gracious Father. Use Jeremiah's lament to learn to channel your grief in a godly way. Do not complain against God, but bring your sorrows to God in prayer. Look to Christ, remembering that as it was with Him so it will be with us: humiliation precedes exaltation (Phil. 2:5–11).

EXERCISING FAITH UNDER HARDSHIP

Jeremiah's deep-seated lamentation now begins to shift toward faith. Like him, Christians must walk by faith in their grief (Lam. 3:19–38). We are thinking and believing Christians, and how we think and what we meditate on during trials largely determines how we bear them by faith in Christ. I once ministered to a man who had recently lost his wife to brain cancer. He received counsel both inside and outside of the church to cut all ties that reminded him of his deceased wife, in spite of the dramatic ways that the church ministered to his family. He sold his home and left his church to go to another church in town. This decision devastated a local congregation that had invested itself heavily in ministering to this man, his wife, and his children in their trials. His actions left a wake of heartache for the man and his children and created a sense of abandonment and betrayal among their friends. The bad counsel he received taught him to turn inward by grieving at the expense of God's glory and the church's profit. This is not the biblical pattern for dealing with grief.[8]

Lamentations 3:1–39 teaches us how to grieve in a godly manner and how to exercise joyful faith in Christ simultaneously. This second section shows us how to exercise faith under grief through prayer, meditation, and humble submission to the Lord.

Turn Our Grief into Prayer (vv. 19–20)

The prophet finally presents the first petition in his lament. The result was not immediately encouraging. Prayer is the soul's outlet to God (Ps. 62:8), but even our prayers can dishearten us at times. Jeremiah prayed, "My soul hath them still in remembrance, and is humbled in me" (Lam. 3:20). Praying over a child's health concerns can remind you that you have no control over your situation and no immediate solution to your problems. While we must still make decisions and call doctors, we are tempted to throw our hands up in despair.

---

8. For excellent and opposite counsel, see Albert N. Martin, *Grieving, Hope and Solace: When a Loved One Dies in Christ* (Adelphi, Md.: Cruciform Press, 2011).

While we must pray in distress, the very exercise of making our requests known to God can drive our sorrow to new depths. Most suffering Christians know this by experience. We sympathize with the psalmist who wrote, "I remembered God, and was troubled: I complained, and my spirit was overwhelmed" (Ps. 77:3). Jeremiah tells us that he prayed for this reason, but he then spends most of his time teaching us how to think and meditate while we pray. Prayer is the first step to exercising joyful faith in Christ under grief. Yet prayer must take direction from meditation on the right truths for the occasion.

Confront Our Grief with Meditation (vv. 21–38)
Exercising faith in distress is often like meeting resistance while lifting weights. Calling the great truths of Scripture to mind, especially truths about God's character, gives us hope. Though the Puritans are best known for their devotional writings, many people fail to recognize that much Puritan application was devoted to meditation and to reconditioning our thinking by it. For example, in John Owen's famous book *The Mortification of Sin*, eight of nine rules for mortification address how to think.[9] Contrary to the cultural assumption that meditation

---

9. John Owen, *The Mortification of Sin*, in *The Works of John Owen*, ed. W. H. Goold (London: Banner of Truth Trust, 1965), 6:chaps. 9–13. Rule 6 urges us to prevent the occasions and advantages of sin. The other eight rules address our thoughts and affections in relation to sin.

involves emptying our minds, biblical meditation involves intense thought and labor.[10] Jeremiah teaches us in Lamentations 3:21–38 how to meditate on seven aspects of God's character and our relation to Him in order to put our prayers on a leash and lead them in the right direction.

The first and primary meditation here is that the Lord's mercies preserve us (Lam. 3:22–23). His mercies express His faithfulness to His covenant promises. The *covenant* refers to our relationship to God as our God in Christ, with the Spirit being the seal of God's covenant promises to us, applying them to us for our salvation. God's mercies are many, and He renews them every morning, as we need new mercies day by day. Thankfully, there are enough divine mercies for the troubles of each day. These verses are the origin of the well-known hymn "Great Is Thy Faithfulness." Yet few people realize that the prophet penned these words in the face of a ruined city where women were eating their children and the nation was in exile. Exodus 34:6–7 is the basis of this profession of faith:

> And the LORD passed by before [Moses], and proclaimed, The LORD, The LORD God, merciful and gracious, longsuffering, and abundant in goodness and truth, keeping mercy for thousands, forgiving iniquity and transgression

---

10. For more information on meditation, see Joel R. Beeke, *How Can I Practice Christian Meditation?*, Cultivating Biblical Godliness (Grand Rapids: Reformation Heritage Books, 2016).

and sin, and that will by no means clear the guilty; visiting the iniquity of the fathers upon the children, and upon the children's children, unto the third and to the fourth generation.

By appealing to who God is from this text, the prophet implied that things could have been worse and should have been worse in light of the curse of sin. God's good character alone brings mercy alongside wrath. We must confront grief with the knowledge that our merciful God preserves His people in the face of distress and in the midst of sin.

Jeremiah's second meditation is that the Lord is our portion (Lam. 3:24; see also Psalms 16, 17, 29, 146). The substance of God's covenant with man is that He will be our God, we will be His people, and He will dwell in our midst (Ex. 6:7; Lev. 26:12). This is why Jesus is called Immanuel, which means God with us (Isa. 7:14; Matt. 1:23). Christ is with His people to the end of the age (Matt. 28:19–20). By uniting us to Christ through the Spirit, God has adopted us as His children, and He has made us joint heirs with Christ (Rom. 8:17). Whatever our subjective circumstances in this world, we should remember we are objectively rich beyond measure. We have received the greater part that will not be taken from us (Luke 10:42). Meditation on God as our portion should lead us to pray for deliverance:

From men which are thy hand, O LORD, from men of the world, which have their portion in this life, and whose belly thou fillest with thy hid treasure: they are full of children, and leave the rest of their substance to their babes. As for me, I will behold thy face in righteousness: I shall be satisfied, when I awake, with thy likeness. (Ps. 17:14–15)

The third thought is that the Lord is good to His people (Lam. 3:25–26). We should probably read the refrain in these verses as "He is good," instead of "it is good."[11] The Lord shows His goodness to those who patiently wait for Him in prayer. Because the Lord is good, we should hope and wait quietly for the salvation of the Lord. This is an exercise in faith rather than a reaction of sense. Hope in prayer must begin with confessing the Lord's goodness. Though He appears to tarry, we must wait for Him (Hab. 2:3).

Fourth, the Lord disciplines those whom He loves (Lam. 3:27–30). We should bear God's yoke, even when He lays it on us in youth (v. 27). As in Lamentations 1:1 Jerusalem was the city sitting alone in silence, so believers should keep silence before God (Hab. 2:20). Being still and knowing that the Lord is God (Ps. 46:10) literally means to stop striving.[12] We must neither despair of our hope nor grumble

---

11. Mackay, *Lamentations: Living in the Ruins*, 145–46.

12. Joseph Alexander treats this text as God's call to the enemies of His people, but regarding it as a call to His people better fits the context. Joseph A. Alexander, *The Psalms Translated and Explained* (Grand Rapids: Baker Book House, 1975), 219.

against God's providences. We must put our mouths in the dust and give our cheeks to those who strike us (Lam. 3:29–30). The parallels to Christ's submission to the Father under His suffering are unmistakable. Yet this is a noisy silence. It is not the silence of inactivity, but the silence of meditative and prayerful submission to God. Our prayers must move through the channels of faith as we submit ourselves to God's fatherly discipline.

The fifth meditation is that the Lord is compassionate to His people (Lam. 3:31–33). The chastisements of the Lord are temporary. He shows compassion toward those whom He grieves, and "He doth not afflict willingly nor grieve the children of men" (v. 33). Though all things come to pass according to the counsel of God's will (Eph. 1:11) and the Lord changes not (Mal. 3:6), He uses the language of human emotions to communicate the depths of His compassion to His people. Isaiah says similarly, "In all their affliction he was afflicted" (Isa. 63:9). This is like the prophet saying that when the Lord chastens His people, His heart is not in it. Affliction does not reflect the end of His purpose for us. Look to God who is like a Father to you and who does not delight as much in chastening His people as in "the peaceable fruit of righteousness" that comes through their trials (Heb. 12:11).

The Lord's just character is the sixth meditation (Lam. 3:34–36). The world is full of injustice. Scoffers cry, "Where is the God of judgment?" (Mal. 2:17). Yet we must grasp divine justice with the hands of faith.

He does not approve those who crush the prisoners of the earth under their feet, who turn aside justice while acting like God does not see, and who "subvert a man in his cause" (Lam. 3:36). He will render to each person according to their deeds (Rom. 2:6). Though the wicked taunt saying, "Where is the promise of his coming?" (2 Peter 3:4), we should remember that "the heavens and the earth, which are now, by the same word are kept in store, reserved unto fire against the day of judgment and perdition of ungodly men" (v. 7). Christ will vindicate those who wait patiently for Him to come from heaven (1 Thess. 1:10).

The final meditation is the one that many well-intended people counsel us to shy away from or to deny. The Lord is in control over all things (Lam. 3:37–38). Nothing comes to pass, whether woe or well-being, that the Lord has not ordered. We live by the command of God's providential word (Deut. 8:3; Matt. 4:4). Some people try to exclude God from catastrophe and moral evil, attempting to protect His character. Others use God's sovereignty over evil as an excuse for unbelief. Yet believers should take refuge in knowing that the Lord who controls all things is merciful, is our portion, is good and does good, disciplines those whom He loves, is compassionate, and is just. This final meditation on God's sovereignty is the capstone of Christian comfort, without which we could have none. He brings meaning, purpose, and salvation out of the greatest hardship (Rom. 8:28) because He brings all things to pass according to the counsel of His will (Eph. 1:11). This is why we are more than conquerors through Him who loved us (Rom. 8:37).

Be Humbled under Grief (v. 39)

Like every other aspect of godly living, grief has proper bounds that we must not transgress. Humility is the proper response to prayer and meditation under grief. Sin is the cause of all grief and sorrow. The Lord may discipline us for personal sin, as He disciplined David, who lost his son for his murder and adultery (2 Sam. 12:18). In such cases, the long-suffering of the Lord leads us to repentance (Rom. 2:4). We also suffer in this life as the consequence of Adam's first sin (Gen. 3:16–19). All who are in Adam die, and all who are in Christ will be made alive (1 Cor. 15:22). Meditation on God's character should remind us that the illness of a child, the loss of a spouse, hurricanes, earthquakes, wars, and other disasters are results of sin. Instead of leading us to complain against God, this should humble us under the mighty hand of God, who resists the proud but gives grace to the humble (James 4:6). Use affliction to confess the corporate sins of the church and of the nation, praying for repentance in both realms. Confess and repent of personal sins. While you may not always suffer for personal sins, your sufferings should be an occasion to repent of personal sins. The same storm that floods the land waters the trees and makes them grow.

How Should We Grieve through Faith in Christ?

On one occasion, I taught my congregation to sing Psalm 102. The tune is mournful, and the words express the depths of believing sorrow. Yet the psalmist ends with hope and praise in light of our eternal and unchangeable covenant-keeping Lord. I told the people that if they did not resonate with this psalm presently, they would need it someday. Sometimes our greatest need as believers is not to subdue and deny our grief but to subject our grief through faith to the triune God. We must submit to the Father's hand in discipline. We must be partakers with Christ in His suffering. We must cultivate the comforts of the Holy Spirit. If we have seen affliction by the rod of His wrath, then we must become people who confess that the Lord's faithfulness is great. This is what Lamentations 3:1–39 teaches us about expressing grief and walking through it by faith in Christ.

WHAT ABOUT WHEN I LOSE A LOVED ONE IN CHRIST?

Some sorrows press us more heavily than others. All Christians have or will struggle with the death of a loved one in Christ. Unless the Lord of glory returns first, wiping away every tear from our eyes, we will weep when the Lord takes away those whom we love. It is vital in such circumstances to have a clearly lit path of faith before us so that we can walk it with Christ through the darkness around us. This final section builds on Jeremiah's example of godly grieving by adding a few meditations and applying them to a particular case. This applies the Bible's general counsel on grieving to a concrete case.

Christ is the fountain of life, and the Spirit is the fountain of living waters; together with the Father they sustain us through every circumstance of life, including losing a loved one. We may struggle with unbelief during these times, especially if the death is sudden, unexpected, and seems untimely. This can be a time of increasing closeness to Christ or a means to drive a wedge between us and the Lord and between us and His people. Ultimately it is not our circumstances that harm us but how we respond to them through faith in Christ. All I can do is pass along to you some of the comfort by which our Father, who is the God of all comforts, has given to me in my afflictions that He will give to you if you wait for Him (2 Cor. 1:3–5).

Christ Is Near to Us in Our Grief

You must think of Christ first and frequently if you hope to pull through this valley of tears. He was a man of sorrows who was acquainted with grief (Isa. 53:3). With every step He took in His life, the wrath and curse of God for our sins weighed on Him with increasing severity, culminating in the cross (Phil. 2:5–8). Every grief He bore removed God's curse from us in all of our grief (Gal. 3:13). He bore all the effects of Adam's fall into sin so that we might be delivered from Adam's fall into sin (Rom. 5:12–20).

He transforms our grief into triumph, makes our suffering instruments of sanctification, changed death into entering His embrace, and will swallow all our sorrows in the resurrection, which He sealed with His own resurrection.

When we moved to California, we lost our daughter, Abigail. A few days later, I preached on "Jesus wept" (John 11:35). This is the shortest verse in the Bible yet one of the most profound. Jesus allowed Lazarus to die because He knew what He was going to do (v. 14). Yet He did not comfort Lazarus's grieving sisters by telling them that Lazarus would rise after being dead for only four days. Instead, He told Martha that He was the resurrection and the life, that those who believe in Him would never die, and even when they die they will live (vv. 25–26). His pointed question to Martha comes to us: "Believest thou this?" She did (v. 27), yet like us she was still overcome by grief. When Jesus saw and heard the people weeping at the tomb, He did not dismiss their grief as unbelief. The Greek text says that "He burned with anger" (v. 33). You might be tempted to be angry when facing the death of those who are close to you. Some of you may even be angry at God for taking someone from you. Jesus shows us that anger in the face of death can be holy. The question is, Why did the Lord burn with anger at the funeral of His friend? Was He angry at God? Surely not. Though Job eventually sinned with his lips and skirted the edge of despair, Jesus never sinned in heart, speech, or behavior. He was angry because death is our "last enemy" (1 Cor. 15:26). Contrary to what some people will tell you, death is not a natural part of life. It is a penalty for sin (Rom. 6:23), which Jesus's people are freed from. Yet we bear the marks of sin in us. We are all dying, including the youngest among us. I am conscious of it every time I pray with my wife and children and every time I preach the gospel. Jesus really wept for His friends and to express His own grief. Like Jesus, be angry before God rather than against God. Be angry at sin and its effects in us and in those we love rather than at the Lord, who redeems His people from their sins.

Jesus raised Lazarus, but Lazarus would die again. So must we all, if Christ does not return first. Eventually, either you must part from all whom you love or they must part from you first. Yet how did Jesus's teaching on Himself as the resurrection and the life transform Lazarus's second funeral— and how will it transform our own? Jesus reminded Martha, as He reminds us, that we must believe that Christ took death and its sorrows on Himself so that we might have abundant life in Him, both now and forever. Jesus grieved deeply with His friends in their sorrow, and He grieved the loss of His friend. Will Jesus abandon believers when they lose those closest to them? Just as Jesus drove His friends to trust Him, so He does with us all. He is a sympathetic high priest whose Father gives us mercy and grace to help in our time of need (Heb. 4:16). He gave us His Word and Spirit to lead us through our grief, and He walks with us through every step of it. Be often in Scripture so that you have anchors for your faith. Look continually to the life of Christ in particular. The risen Lord brought my wife and me through the death of a daughter and Lazarus's family through the death of a brother; He will bring you through the death of your loved ones.

Death Is from the Lord

The difficult part of this is moving from fear and even anger to faith. We must face these realities rather than flee from them. The remedy is to remember who the Lord is and who He has revealed Himself to be in Christ. We must trust the Spirit, that great Comforter, to use these things to strengthen our hearts. In the midst of Job's grief, God did not explain to Job why He did what He did; rather, He revealed His glory to Job (Job 38–41). We need to see God's glory as well. In order to do so, we should study the Bible prayerfully, asking what it teaches us about God on every page. Job's example, though vital, does not give us the full picture. God revealed his glory to Job without further explaining the reasons for his suffering. We have even greater comfort available to us as we meditate on how our sovereign God deals with us in Christ.

The character of Christ in dealing with His disciples struck me most powerfully when I learned that a close friend was dying. When I heard the news, I was reading Matthew 14. After feeding the five thousand, in which Jesus showed His power to provide for and satisfy all His disciples' needs, He walked on water. His disciples were alone in the boat and were terrified at the storm about them. When they saw Jesus walking on water, their fear increased, thinking that He was a ghost. He responded, "Be of good cheer; it is I; be not afraid" (Matt. 14:27). Peter took courage for a moment and asked to come to the Lord on the water. Yet when he saw the wind and the waves, he began to sink. But it was the same Jesus who walked on the sea who stood with Peter on the water, which led Jesus to say, "O thou of little faith, wherefore didst thou doubt?" (v. 31). Before they knew it, the boat was on land.

What was the Lord's point? No matter the circumstances, we know and confess with our hearts that it is from the Lord. This observation moves beyond the context a little, but nevertheless it speaks powerfully to who the Lord is. The disciples moved, in the end, from a great trial and many fears to confess that Jesus was the Son of God (Matt. 14:33). His presence in the trial is what matters. He is just as in control over your loved one's death as He was over the storm and the sea that day. While Jesus glorified God by healing a man born blind, He told Peter that he would glorify God in his death (John 21:19). He could have prevented Peter's death, and He could have left the man in his blindness. He is the God who brings all things to pass according to the counsel of his will (Eph. 1:11). No one speaks or brings anything to pass that the Lord has not ordered (Lam. 3:37–38). We need both God's sovereignty over our afflictions and Christ's presence in our afflictions to press through them. God's sovereignty gives us hope in His wisdom and purpose, which we rarely understand beyond the general truth that all things work for His glory and our salvation (Rom. 8:28). God's presence in Christ by the Spirit enables us to see Him in the midst of the storm. You may never know in this life why the Lord took your loved one when He did, but you must believe that the Lord is still with you. He will never leave us nor forsake us. We must know and believe that Jesus, the Son of God, is the Lord of the storm, who either delivers us from our trials or carries us through them. In either case, we must know that it is the Lord who stands behind all these things. If we lose sight of this, then the heavy burdens we bear will threaten to crush us.

With respect to the deaths of believers, Al Martin reminds us as well that Christ prayed that His people would be with Him where He is. He writes, "If that loved one belonged to Jesus, then death serves as the means for Jesus to receive the desire of his heart."[13] The deaths of believers are from the Lord, and their purpose is more about the Lord than about us. Martin quotes Spurgeon as saying,

---

13. Martin, *Grieving, Hope and Solace*, 71.

Every time a believer mounts from this earth
to paradise, it is an answer to Christ's prayer.
A good old divine remarks, "Many times Jesus
and his people pull against one another in
prayer. You bend your knee and say, Father, I
will that Thy saints be with me where I am";
Christ says, "Father, I will that they also, whom
Thou hast given Me, be with Me where I am."...
Now, which pleader shall win the day?[14]

When we recognize that the death of our loved ones
comes from the Lord, we are reminded that Christ's
desire and plan for them is better than ours. This
helps shift our focus from ourselves to them and
to God.

Grieve Rather than Stifle Grief

Expressing grief properly reflects the first part of
Lamentations 3. Many of the psalms and the entire
book of Lamentations are dedicated to this point
exclusively. It is important to add here that while we
must grieve, we must not do so like the unbelieving
world (1 Thess. 4:13). We must not sorrow as those
who have no hope, yet we must sorrow. Our hearts
must vent themselves in words. We must talk about
our departed loved one with others, but we must
talk about him and our grief in losing him to God
most of all. If we do not use God's words to grieve
as in the Psalms and Lamentations, then we will be

---

14. As quoted in Martin, *Grieving, Hope and Solace*, 45–46.

left to our own words. Some of what we think, say, and feel will be right, but some things will be wrong. It is vital to remember that the Scriptures give us channels by which we can vent our hearts and let our grief flow. We need this desperately. This is part of how the Spirit comforts us in Christ through our trials. As we grieve, we must meditate on Christ's sorrows for us so that we can experience the Spirit's comfort in us.

Do Not Be Alone
In the Psalms, one of David's greatest trials was that his friends and loved ones left him. Yet he knew that even if this were the case, the Lord would take care of him (Ps. 27:10). Christ trod the winepress of God's wrath alone (Isa. 63:3), and He was forsaken by God (Ps. 22:1), by the crowds, and by His friends at the cross. Even His familiar friend Judas, with whom He shared His bread, turned his heel against Him and betrayed Him (Ps. 41:9). Peter denied Him before a servant girl. Only John went to the cross at the end. Being alone under the crushing weight of grief adds stones to our backs, threatening that we will sink into despair.

Yet you are not alone. Do not let yourself be alone. You have the church and friends in the Lord who love you. Most of them will not know how to help you. Many will keep their distance, thinking you need time. They will likely tend to give you space and leave you alone. Don't let yourself get lost in your grief. A dear friend of ours had a terrible marriage. Her husband was converted suddenly, and they had one year of a great marriage until he died just as suddenly of an aggressive cancerous tumor. Soon afterward, she shut herself in the house and did not go out. We eventually encouraged her to start having dinner with our family regularly and to go on walks with our children. We invited others into our home to be with her as well, and friends brought her to church. Being with others pulled her back to solid Christian fellowship, and light began to shine through the darkness. Christ is all you need in every circumstance of life, but Christ is present with His people, and He ministers to us through them. Paul was refreshed by the presence of Titus, Jesus called His closest friends to pray with Him in Gethsemane, and we need God's people in our struggles with despair. In short, we need the church, and we should be thankful in every circumstance of life that God does not ordinarily call us to live the Christian life alone.

CONCLUSION

Grieving is a reality in a sin-cursed world. We must learn to express our grief in godly ways rather than to suppress it. We must learn what to meditate on in order to walk through grief by faith. We must struggle against the temptation to look to ourselves and our circumstances too much. Look to Christ in His sufferings for you. Trust in the living Christ so that you might live in Him. Talk to older, mature Christians in your church, some of whom may have lost spouses or children and endured other hardships, and ask them to help you. Expect to hear Christ's voice in the preaching of the Word and to see Him and meet Him at the Lord's Table. If you have not yet come to the Lord's Table, then use your loved one's death to drive you into Christ's arms and to confess your faith in Him openly. Remember the promises that the triune God gave you in your baptism. Take God as your Father, Jesus as your Savior, and the Spirit as your Comforter. Commend yourself and others to God and to the word of His grace (Acts 20:32). He can offer comfort to you beyond any other counselor.